Views from our Shoes

Growing Up

with a Brother or Sister

with Special Needs

Edited by Donald Meyer

Illustrated by Cary Pillo

Woodbine House   1997

© 1997 Donald J. Meyer

All rights reserved under International and Pan-American copyright conventions. Published in the United States of America by Woodbine House, Inc., 6510 Bells Mill Rd., Bethesda, MD 20817. 800-843-7323.

Cover & inside illustrations by: Cary Pillo

Library of Congress Cataloging-in-Publication Data

Views from our shoes : growing up with a brother or sister with special needs / edited by Donald J. Meyer.
    p. cm.
  ISBN 0-933149-98-0
  1. Developmentally disabled children—United States—Family relationships. 2. Brothers and sisters—United States. I. Meyer, Donald J. (Donald Joseph), 1951-
HV894.V54 1997
362.1'968—dc21   97-18351
                                                    CIP

Manufactured in the United States of America

10 9 8 7 6 5

In the United States, there are over four million people who have developmental disabilities. Most of these people have brothers and sisters.

This book is for them.

About the Editor

Donald Meyer is the director of the Sibling Support Project located at Children's Hospital and Medical Center in Seattle. As director, Don conducts workshops on sibling issues for parent and professional audiences throughout the United States and Canada and training sessions on how to start Sibshops, educational and support programs for school-age brothers and sisters. Sibshops now exist in about 33 states and two Canadian provinces. Don is also the editor of *UNCOMMON FATHERS* (Woodbine House, 1995) and co-author of *SIBSHOPS: WORKSHOPS FOR BROTHERS AND SISTERS OF CHILDREN WITH SPECIAL NEEDS* (P.H. Brookes, 1994); and *LIVING WITH A BROTHER OR SISTER WITH SPECIAL NEEDS* (University of Washington Press, 1996) He is currently working on a book for grandparents of children with special needs. Don and his wife, Terry, a preschool special education teacher, live with their four children in Seattle.

Table of Contents

A Note to Readers vii
Acknowledgements ix

Views from . . .
    Ben Stephenson, 4 1
    Amber Catford-Robinson, 5 3
    Michelle Grantin, 6 5
    Erica Stevenson, 6 7
    Arielle Eva Cohen, 7 8
    Ryan Kurtz, 7 9
    Elizabeth Alar, 7 10
    Nick Pawelkiewicz, 8 11
    Chris Curtland, 8 12
    Brandon Urban, 8 15
    Stephanie Sochia, 8 17
    Jennifer Praino, 8 19
    Angela Sorrem, 8 21
    Lizzie Suwala, 9 23
    Michelle Dodd, 9 25
    Jessica Kolber, 9 27
    Annelih Holganza, 9 29
    Lorielle Fiedler, 10 31
    Steven Meade, 10 33
    Ryan Clearwater, 10 35
    Justin Faulkingham, 10 37
    Sarah Lowry, 10 39
    Helen Rittelmeyer, 10 41
    Chelsea Brown, 11 43
    Matt Sochia, 11 45

Stephanie Hodge, 11 47
Alisha Axman, 11 49
Crystal Marie Kirstein, 11 51
Lauren Siber, 11 52
Justin Mann, 12 53
Jaci Raia, 12 57
Michelle Newman, 12 59
Joe Hockaday, 12 61
Allison Hansen, 12 63
Diana Lowe, 13 65
Jeanne Marie Pinto, 13 67
Justin Boraas, 13 71
Derek Urban, 13 73
Anne Meade, 14 75
Katie Suwala, 14 77
Severn Kraut, 14 79
Amy Pogue, 14 81
Joshua Kaplan, 16 83
Megan Patterson, 17 87
Kate Turnbull, 18 90

So What's on Your Mind? 95
Appendix
    About the World Wide Web 99
    Organizations Serving People with
        Special Needs 100
    Information for Siblings 105
Glossary 106
Index 114

A Note to Readers

Dear Readers:

I'll admit it: I love my job. In my work, I help start Sibshops, which are truly fun programs just for brothers and sisters of kids who have special needs. At Sibshops, kids meet other brothers and sisters and play lots of "new games." We laugh a lot, and talk about life with our brothers or sisters. Kids who come to Sibshops say it is good to know that what happens to them sometimes happens to other kids too.

Another great part of my job is that I get to meet many, many brothers and sisters. I always remind them that they are experts. That is, they know more about being the sibling (brother or sister) of a person with special needs than most adults ever will. I also tell them that, because they are experts, they have a lot to teach people.

Although more and more communities now have Sibshops, there still aren't enough. I wanted to create a book for kids who have never been to a Sibshop. This book would give them a chance to "meet" other brothers and sisters. I wanted them to be able to read about other siblings' thoughts and experiences. It can help to know that others sometimes feel the way you feel. And I wanted this book to help parents and others understand what having a sibling with special needs is all about.

To create this book, I invited young people from across the United States to write and tell me about their lives with their brothers and sisters. I told them I wanted to hear it all—the good stuff, the not-so-good stuff, and everything in between. As I think you will agree, they have done just that!

On the pages of *Views from Our Shoes,* you will find the thoughts of 45 brothers and sisters. Their ages range from 4 to 18 and they live in 18 different states. Their siblings have many different types of special needs, including: autism, cerebral palsy, developmental delays, health problems, attention deficit disorder, hydrocephalus, mental retardation, visual and hearing impairments, and Down, Angelman, Mohr, Tourette, and Rett syndromes.

One final note to the grown-ups who read this book. One of the real joys of my work is listening to the frequently thoughtful observations that brothers and sisters make at Sibshops. The wisdom and insights I have heard these young participants share may also be found in the essays contained in *Views from Our Shoes* I hope you will find these young authors' thoughts and observations as valuable as I do!

All the best,
Don Meyer
Director, Sibling Support Project
Children's Hospital and Medical Center
Seattle, Washington

Acknowledgements

Creating *Views from Our Shoes* was, from the very start, a labor of love. I have been lucky to have had enthusiastic help as I realized my dream of bringing the common-sense validation found at a Sibshop to book form. Along the way, I have had help from:

❖ The many Sibshop and sibling program coordinators from across the United States who encouraged their young participants to share their thoughts with us;

❖ Kari Ciaciuch and Helen Read of the Sibling Support Project who helped keep track of our many contributors;

❖ Hillary Stockwell, volunteer extraordinaire, for her considerable keyboarding skills;

❖ Children's Hospital and Medical Center and the U.S. Department of Education for their support and belief in the work of the Sibling Support Project;

❖ Cynthia Shurtleff, Sue Levi-Pearl, and Krishni Patrick, who assured that our brief descriptions of disabilities were correct;

❖ Patricia Vadasy and Gina Meyer for being fine sounding boards (again!);

❖ Ryan Medlen and Jesse Shapell, young sibling reviewers who critiqued the manuscript and encouraged Woodbine House to publish *Views from Our Shoes;*

❖ Cary Pillo for gracing these pages with her illustrations;

❖ the parents of the contributors who allowed their children to speak from the heart—even if what they said might be difficult for them to hear;

❖ and most of all, to the young brothers and sisters who generously shared what was in their hearts and minds.

I am grateful to all!

Ben Stephenson, 4

My Mommy and Daddy told me that Nicole was born very early and her brain got hurt. I love Nicole. I like to hug her.

I like it when Nathan comes in his truck to fill Nicole's oxygen tank. I also like Nicole's nurses. They take care of her and they play with me! When Nicole's school bus comes, sometimes I get to sit on the driver's seat. I like to go to Nicole's school. Her teacher said I could ride their horse at school when it is summer.

I like to push Nicole's wheelchair when we go for walks. In the winter I shovel snow off her ramp. Nicole walks with her walker if you help her. I like to play with Nicole's walker. I tie it to my car.

Nicole chews and tears everything! I don't like that. She is very messy when she eats. Sometimes Nicole wakes me up at night. I don't like that either.

I really don't like it when Nicole gets sick. When

Nicole had a seizure, she had to go to the hospital for a little while. An ambulance came to take her to the hospital. They invited me to look in the ambulance. I liked that!

Nicole will still be handicapped when she gets bigger. Her brain won't get better. Nurses and Mom and Dad will take care of Nicole.

To say "I love you" Nicole says "goo!" She doesn't know how to talk yet. Nicole loves me. She doesn't know, but I do know that.

2

Ben lives in Hudsonville, Michigan and likes cars, building with blocks, make-believe, tigers, and bears. His sister Nicole, 8, has cerebral palsy, chronic lung disease, and seizures. ✰

✰ *What's cerebral palsy? Turn to page 107 to find out! To find out more about seizures, turn to page 112.*

Amber Catford-Robinson, 5

My sister's name is Naomi and my name is Amber. I am five and she is three. We think Naomi has Rett syndrome ✱ and some other things.

✱ Find out more about Rett syndrome by turning to page 111!

I like to play with Naomi. If she cries, I can make her laugh by laughing! Naomi has an electric piano. Sometimes I move her arms and help her push the keys to make music. I love to play with her. She loves me best of all.

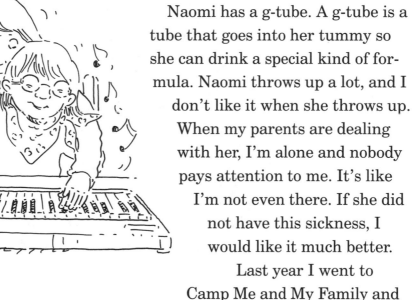

Naomi has a g-tube. A g-tube is a tube that goes into her tummy so she can drink a special kind of formula. Naomi throws up a lot, and I don't like it when she throws up. When my parents are dealing with her, I'm alone and nobody pays attention to me. It's like I'm not even there. If she did not have this sickness, I would like it much better.

Last year I went to Camp Me and My Family and met some new friends who have sisters and brothers with special needs. We had a lot of fun! One girl had a

3

brother who has a g-tube and was in a wheelchair and couldn't talk, just like Naomi.

If Naomi didn't have special needs, I would be much happier. Thinking of all the things we could do together fills up my brain with thoughts! We would do all sorts of things—play ball, make up games together, or play in the hot tub.

When we go to school, I sometimes like to bring Naomi into my classroom and introduce her to my classmates. Sometimes, if we are early enough, I go into her classroom and see her classmates.

I worry about Naomi sometimes. When she is in school I wonder what she is doing and if she is having a good day. When I get home from school, I can't wait to see the art she did at school.

On weekends I like friends to come over to play and meet Naomi.

I wish she will get better sometime in her life. But I do not wish she will get better in days, weeks, months, or years. I just wish she would get better the minute I wish it.

Amber, who loves to dance, swim, swing, rollerskate, and read, lives in Forestville, California.

4

Michelle Grantin, 6

My name is Michelle. I'm 6 years old. My brother Aaron
is 5. He has special needs, like autism.✴ It is fun playing with him. I enjoy reading to him. Our favorite
books are Morning Town Ride and Boxcar Children
and Goosebumps. We even look at books in bed.

*Michelle lives in Oregon, Wisconsin and enjoys danc-
ing and paleontology.*

✴ *Turn to page 106 to learn about autism!*

Erica Stevenson, 6

Jake, my sister J.C., and I like to play in the pool. We splash around and have fun. But I don't like it when Jake scratches me when nobody is watching and then runs away.

I do like it when Jake comes to my room and we play with my toys. But I don't like it when he makes Mommy and Daddy mad, because Mommy screams and yells. It hurts my feelings when that happens.

I get mad when Jake draws on my walls and makes dark marks on them. Mommy cleans it up. If I did that *I* would have to clean it up! But I guess it's all right that Jake doesn't have to clean up because he doesn't understand.

Erica lives in New Windsor, New York. Her brother, Jacob, is 5 and has autism. ✵

✵ *What's autism? Turn to page 106 to find out!*

Arielle Eva Cohen, 7

My brother's name is Zachary Benjamin Cohen. He has special needs. I am an expert on calling 911 because when my brother was very sick I got scared and really thought he was going to die. I remember feeling scared, frightened, and then a little bit mad because my Mom and Dad spent a lot of time at the children's hospital.

Because he is not a typical kid, Zachary gets a lot of attention. I need attention too because I am the middle child. It can be hard on me some times.

Arielle lives in Scottsdale, Arizona. She enjoys art, gymnastics, and riding bikes. Her brother, Zachary, is 6 and has an autonomic nervous system disorder. ✹ *To see what their brother Joshua wrote, turn to page 83.*

✹ Autonomic nervous system disorder is defined on page 107!

Ryan Kurtz, 7

It is not so easy to have a brother who has a disability. I love him, but sometimes I do not like what he does to me. Sometimes he grabs me hard and screams for no reason. I say I hate him sometimes but I really do love him very, very much. Sometimes I hug him. He's a very nice kid. Who cares if he has a disability? I like him.

★ Find out more about hydrocephalus by turning to page 110!

Ryan lives in Delmont, Pennsylvania, and likes to play hockey, videogames, and baseball. His brother, Doug, 19, has hydrocephalus.★

Elizabeth Alar, 7

I think Matt's different than me because his brain is arranged different. He often acts like having me around bothers him. Sometimes he doesn't let me see what he's doing. Some kids at school say I don't have a brother because he's autistic. Having autism✭ makes Matt act kind of strange.

✭ Autism, see page 106.

I can't really talk with Matt, but I can ask him questions. Whenever I try to start a conversation by saying his name, he says "WHAT!!" It's kind of like he's yelling at me. He doesn't like to talk to me and he doesn't want to answer my questions.

Matt is really smart. He goes to a regular high school and gets mostly As and Bs on his report cards. He is also on the math team and got the 7th highest score in the whole state of Wisconsin on the American High School Math Exam.

I like Matt and I care about him a lot. I think he cares about me too, because he gets really upset if he thinks I might be hurt. Sometimes I worry about what will happen to him when he grows up because he might not know how to take care of himself.

Liz lives in Cottage Grove, Wisconsin. Her interests include cats and her friends. Her brother, Matt, is 17.

Nick Pawelkiewicz, 8

My brother, Brad, has cerebral palsy✷ and can't walk without a walker. Sometimes my mom says I can't go out to play because Brad might feel left out.

I think that when my brother Brad grows up he will be able to walk—but just not the same way we walk. He might have to use a wheelchair when he goes to Great America or the zoo or the circus. He would be able to get out of the chair to get in line for Great America or to pet the animals at the petting zoo.

One good thing about Brad having cerebral palsy is that I have learned to be patient. Before Brad came along, I had no patience! We have to slow down and take our time when we are out, because Brad can't walk as fast as us. It helps me be patient with other people, too. There was a girl in my class who couldn't talk and I learned how to deal with her difficulty.

I wish Brad did not have cerebral palsy, but I would rather have Brad with cerebral palsy than no Brad at all!

✷ *Cerebral palsy, see page 107.*

11

Nick lives in Roselle, Illinois, and enjoys hockey, in-line skating, baseball, and swimming. His brother, Brad, is 3 years old.

Chris Curtland, 8

I'm Chris Curtland. I'm 8 years old and in the second grade. My brother's name is Ben Curtland. He's 10 years old and in the fourth grade. My brother uses a wheelchair because he has cerebral palsy.<star /> Ben doesn't get made fun of in school—he's really a cool kid. Boys at school think Ben's neat because he's in a wheelchair and walks in a walker.

When I was two I learned the word balance and more about Ben's disability. I stood up in my highchair and said "I don't have any balance." I thought Ben's disability was called balance! Then my mom explained cerebral palsy to me.

I like being Ben's brother because he can't hurt me when we fight—even though he is older than me! When we grow up I really hope Ben learns to walk because I want him to have the experience of walking without a walker. The Stoney Point Y lets Ben get on a basketball team. Last year he was on the Spurs, this year he is on the Jazz. We have two basketball hoops outside. One's little and one's big. We enjoy playing with each other.

Cerebral palsy, see page 107.

12

If I wasn't Ben's brother I would like being Ben's friend. Around school and in the halls Ben and I give each other high fives. Ben's a neat brother. I love Ben and I know he loves me.

Chris enjoys collecting cards and playing basketball. He lives in Robins, Iowa.

14

Brandon Urban, 8

My name is Brandon Urban. I am 8 years old. My brother Todd is 17. He has autism✹ and doesn't talk. A lot of people say that my brother is retarded. I really do not like that! When I grow up I will take care of him. Even though he is autistic, I love him! When I need help he always helps me.

One thing that I don't like is when he does bad stuff, like when he smeared peanut butter on the wall. My other brother Derek, 13, and I go to a sibling program once a year where we swim and eat ice cream sundaes.

15

Brandon lives in Munhall, Pennsylvania and collects rocks and coins. To read what his brother Derek wrote, see page 73.

✹ *Autism, see page 106.*

Stephanie Sochia, 8

Even though my sister, Amy, has Down syndrome⭐ she is not different from other people. She is the same as other people because she talks and hears and learns new things. I am sure my sister loves me a lot because she waits for me in the window. It makes me mad when people make fun of Amy. I tell them to STOP picking on her and they stop! My friend Caleb has a little brother with Down syndrome and Caleb is lucky too! People with Down syndrome love everything.

17

⭐ *What's Down syndrome? Turn to page 108 to find out.*

Stephanie, who lives in Carthage, New York, likes to ride her bike and collect posters. Her sister, Amy, is 6. The thoughts of their brother, Matt, may be found on page 45.

Jennifer Praino, 8

I found out about Larry's disability last year when I was in second grade. He has Attention Deficit Disorder.★ Larry is very hard to live with. If he doesn't get what he wants he'll throw a fit. If his food isn't fixed the way he likes it he'll throw a fit. He doesn't like anyone doing anything he doesn't like.

★ Turn to page 106 to find out more about Attention Deficit Disorder.

If I go over to my friend's house he'll follow me to her house even though he says he doesn't want to play because he's tired. My Mom and I have to tell him all the time not to go into my room, but he doesn't listen. He's very annoying—even to his own classmates! His classmates are just like him. Larry gets into trouble every day—well most likely every day. When he gets angry he'll trash the house and start to hit my mom or dad or me. If I'm watching something on TV and I have the remote he'll try to get it from me and we'll start to fight.

19

Jennifer lives in Monroe, New York, and likes to play dodge ball and soccer. Her brother, Larry, is 10.

Angela Sorrem, 8

I'm thrilled to be asked to help with the book you're creating! I hope you'll like my ideas. I don't mean to brag or anything, but I'd say I'm pretty excellent when it comes to writing and spelling. Which, of course, is good for your book.

Here are some of my thoughts:

My own sister can be a pain. We get along okay and everything, but we're not the closest sisters we could ever be. Right before her birthday, Carolyn began to realize that not everything in her body worked right. So, a couple nights before her B-day she signed to me "I want new eyes, and ears that work."

Being the sister of a child with special needs can be hard. I know it's hard on any kid with a situation like mine, but there are times when I sit down and think "It's not fair!" And sometimes it isn't fair, but it's just one of those stressful, unfair moments you have to get over and then just move on.

My sister goes to a special school where they provide special care and well-trained physical and occupational therapists. This next year, my sister will be going into first grade, which will be much harder than regular, fun kindergarten. At first, my parents were worried that first grade would be too hard, but I'm sure Carolyn can handle it if she tries. She'll just have to work hard. My family has faith in her, and she has faith in herself.

Every weekend our family has fun times together going to our grandfather's lake cottage. Carolyn has a great time swimming (her favorite sport) and doing all sorts of fun things.

Hope I helped!

Angela lives in Milwaukee, Wisconsin, and likes to swim, tube, read, and play basketball. Her sister Carolyn, 6, is deaf and has a visual impairment and a physical disability.

Lizzie Suwala, 9

When I was in Mrs. Callas's fourth grade room, we had to write about a special person in our life. Of course, I picked my brother, Jason, who is blind, deaf, and mentally retarded. When my teacher chose the top five essays, mine was one of them. Here are some of the things I wrote in my story:

Jason is special to me because he has a disability and is different from other people. Since he's been born he has not been able to see, hear, walk, or talk. I know he is a gifted person, because he got communion when he was 18 years old, and he received it on my sister's birthday.

I watch Jason when my mom is doing things around the house. I hold him on my lap and hug him because he is so little. Sometimes I give him his Prosobee drink after supper. I taught Jason to drink by himself. I don't like it when he pulls my hair, but he doesn't understand.

I also don't like it when people stare at Jason in the store—especially older kids who should know better. (I still think my brother is handsome!) Another thing I don't like is that we can't go on vacations except when Jason goes to summer school. Also, we can't go out to eat because he can only eat certain foods.

My friends aren't a problem, and I am not embarrassed by Jason. My mom took Jason to my class on the last day of school. My teacher wanted to meet him and the kids thought he was cute. I felt happy and proud of him because he didn't cry at all. I like when he goes to church with us because he isn't any problem, except for his noise-making and crying.

I think Jason has helped my sister and me like each other better. Jason is a great brother, and life would be hard to imagine without him. I feel bad for him sometimes because his girlfriend, Michelle, died. They always held hands in class. I wish someday he would be normal like me so I could see what he would be like.

24

Lizzie lives in Ford City, Pennsylvania and likes basketball and softball. To read what her sister, Katie, wrote, *turn to page 77.*

Michelle Dodd, 9

Hi! My name is Michelle and I have a brother who has Down syndrome.✸ When you have Down syndrome, you have an extra chromosome. Down syndrome is something you have before you are born. When you have Down syndrome, you learn slower than other kids. It is nothing anyone can change or be ashamed of. Kids with Down syndrome like the same things you and I like. They like to ride bikes, swim, and have friends.

✸ Down syndrome, see page 108.

My brother's name is Erick and even though he has Down syndrome I still love him. He is one year old. He goes to therapy and day care. He is even beginning to crawl! I make the most time for him I can. When we are together, we like to play with his toys and we like to play with our dog, Tanner. Erick makes us all very happy.

25

Since my brother was born, I've learned a lot of things about Down syndrome. I've gone to Sibshops ✸ and talked with children who have brothers and sisters with special needs. I have also met other kids who have brothers and sisters with special needs on the Internet. One girl, Julie, lives in New York. We write back and forth to each other on our computers. We write about problems, how we can solve them, about my brother and her sister.

26

Michelle lives in North Plainfield, New Jersey, and loves softball, gymnastics, swimming, camping, reading, and riding her bike. Her brother, Erick, is 17 months old.

✸ *Sibshops are fun! Find out what they are on pages 105 and 112.*

Jessica Kolber, 9

My brother, Danny, is 14 years old and has autism.✯ When I was little he bit and pinched me. But now he's a lot better and doesn't do that anymore.

He's pretty nice, but sometimes he's a bit annoying. He repeats certain words, which is called echolalia. We can't keep drinks in the refrigerator because he empties anything in the refrigerator into the sink. He moves my things to different places because, from his point of view, everything should be in a straight line. He goes to our local junior high and is integrated in a few classes, such as ceramics and P.E.

I know I could trust certain friends in telling them about my brother's disability, but it would embarrass me.

In some ways my life is different from kids who have a normal brother, because most of my schedule revolves around Danny. Sometimes I can't go to special activities because my mother has no one to watch Danny and can't take me. I think parents, teachers, and doctors should have more understanding for siblings, because they go through difficult experiences with their brothers or sisters.

When my brother grows up my parents will try to keep him at home for as long as they can. But if they

✯ Autism, see page 106.

27

can't, I'm almost positive he will be in supported living⭐ or a group home. When I grow up I will go to work and have a life of my own. I will visit him each week on Saturday or Sunday to make sure he is OK and to spend time with him.

My advice to other brothers and sisters who have a sib with a disability is:

- ◆ It's tough sometimes, but you get through it.
- ◆ They might act up in ways you don't understand when you're little.
- ◆ If they hurt you, don't get mad because they don't know any better.
- ◆ If they do certain things that annoy you, try to ignore it or go into another room.
- ◆ If they're angry, try to stay out of their way.

Jessica likes to draw, read, and swim. She lives in Valencia, California.

⭐ *Supported living is defined on page 112!*

Annelih Holganza, 9

What I like about having a sister with special needs is that I can help her. I help my sister hold things like rattles and soft small balls. I also help her make sounds on the keyboard, which she really enjoys. I like to make her smile. I also like to go to her school and help her with her school work. It can be fun to have a sister with special needs.

What I don't like about having a sister with special needs is that she can't get things for herself. Sometimes, when I am tired and about to go to sleep Mama says "Annie get a diaper!" I don't like it when Hanna arches because it is very bad for her back. Also I don't like it when we have to suction her lungs because if she has a different color secretion she might be sick and have to go to the hospital. These are some of the things that I don't like about having a sister with special needs!

Annie lives in Everett, Washington. She enjoys reading, dancing, singing, and basketball. Her twin sister, Hanneli, 9, has cerebral palsy.✸

30

✸ *Cerebral palsy, see page 107.*

Lorielle Fiedler, 10

One good thing about being an older sister of a child with special needs is that I am one of my brother's best friends and he loves me very much. The bad thing about having a brother with special needs is that when he gets mad, he blames me for everything and my parents always believe him. He also learns slower and you have to teach him everything.

Kids at school used to say things about my brother like "he can't run fast" or "he talks funny." We're homeschooled now, and nobody in our neighborhood teases him.

The advice that I would give to a brother or sister of a child with special needs is to be kind, patient, and to teach them everything that you know.

I have noticed that my brother acts differently with different friends. For instance, my brother is obnoxious when my friend Hannah comes over, because Hannah is not very nice to him. But when friends come over who are nice to my brother, he acts sweet and calm.

Although my brother has problems, he is very good at reading my thoughts! For instance, if I was thinking "hurry up!" he would say "Stop hurrying me!"

My brother shares a lot with me—he likes things to be fair. One time when we went to Toobtown he got a free soda and shared half of it with me—he even got my favorite flavor, rootbeer. He also likes to pretend to be twins with me, which means the same food, same colors, and the same drinks.

Another thing about my brother is that when he has his mind set on something he usually gets it! Once he saved his money for a radio he wanted. After he got the radio, he wanted me to sing with him. I never thought that it would be so much fun! We pretended we were teenage rock stars!

32

Lorielle lives in Santa Rosa, California, and likes to swim and ride horses. Her brother, Andrew, 8, has Prader-Willi syndrome. ⭐

⭐ *What's Prader-Willi syndrome?*
Page 111 tells you!

Steven Meade, 10

My name is Steven Meade. I am 10 years old. I have a twin; her name is Kristin and she has cerebral palsy.

Cerebral palsy is damage to the brain that affects how her muscles work. Kristin did not get cerebral palsy from getting in a car accident or anything like that—she was just born that way. Kristin had to have a shunt put in to drain extra fluid around her brain.

Kristin has had three surgeries to help her walk better. She had her first surgery when she was six. She

Cerebral palsy, see page 107.

had to wear a big purple cast from her waist to her toes for six weeks.

Kristin and I go to the same school now, but we didn't always. She went to another school for a special program. We are going into the fifth grade.

Even though we fight a lot, we've had some pretty good times. You know, there are some good parts about having a sister with a disability. For instance, when we went to Disneyworld we got to use the handicapped entrance instead of waiting in line for rides and shows.

So, as you can see, Kristin and I have some good times and not-so-good times. But we really do love each other. I think other brothers and sisters all over the world love each other whether they have special needs or not.

Steven likes to fish and ride his bike. He and Kristin live in Levittown, Pennsylvania.

34

Ryan Clearwater, 10

My name is Ryan Clearwater. I am 10 years old. My sister, Lindsey, is 13 years old. She has mental retardation. I would like to share some thoughts I have with you for your book.

Lindsey comes to Shepard school with me and I feel O.K. about that. She sometimes is in a regular class and other times is in a special class. I *don't* feel O.K. when people make fun of Lindsey. It makes me mad and sad at the same time. My good friends understand.

One good time I remember is when I had to read a book to Lindsey at school to make her feel better because someone hurt her feelings on purpose. Reading the book to her calmed her down and I felt good that she was O.K. and safe. I think having a sister with disabilities has made me a more caring and sensitive person.

Lindsey is my only sibling. It is hard to put into words what having a sister with special needs is like, but I can't imagine having a plain old sister. Sometimes I wish she wasn't handicapped—but she is and I can't change that or cure her.

I like to hear Lindsey laugh. I don't like it when Lindsey cries or gets in trouble. Sometimes I'm scared for Lindsey because I can't predict what she will do next. She's in her own little world. Lindsey is a "free spirit" and likes to wander around our neighborhood. We have a fence around my house to keep her safe.

Sometimes I'm jealous of Lindsey. When I ignore my parent's directions, I always get privileges taken away. When Lins ignores them, she doesn't always get punished because she is still learning right from wrong.

When I grow up I want to be involved in sports. When Lindsey grows up I want her to have a job that she enjoys.

Ryan, who likes cards, video games, coin collecting, and sports, lives in Columbia, Missouri.

Justin Faulkingham, 10

My family didn't know that my brother has autism until he was two. After that, my parents read lots of books about autism and my Mom told me about what she read.

My life is a little bit different from other kids my age. Most people I meet don't have brothers or sisters who have problems. There are good parts about having a brother who has autism.✹ My brother, Jacob, is old enough to play with, and he understands some things. But, unfortunately, there is a bad part. Sometimes my brother gets out of hand and hits people—even me!

I'm sure glad he doesn't go to my school, for a number of reasons. First, if Jake needs something he'll scream until he gets it. Second, everybody would know how much of a dope he is. And if they find out that he's my brother, they'd laugh!

I like my brother just the way he is. Even though there are bad parts, there are good parts. I'm glad to have a nice brother to care about me. And I care about him.

Justin, who enjoys playing videogames, lives in Winsor, New York. His brother, Jacob, is 5 years old.

✹ *Autism, see page 106.*

Sarah Lowry, 10

My family likes to go on ski trips. Once, not very long ago, my brother and I were skiing ahead of my Dad. We took a wrong turn on to the black diamond (expert!) run. I started down the hill thinking Jeff was following me—but he wasn't! He had just quietly sat down in the snow. When I got to the bottom, Jeff wasn't there and my dad blamed me! I tried to explain that I thought Jeff was following me, but Dad still got mad! It's not fair. If that happened to me, Jeff wouldn't have gotten in trouble. My dad wanted me to be Jeff's baby-sitter. But I'm younger than Jeff!

39

I have a suggestion for anybody else who gets the blame: tell your parents what you think—but don't yell! If they don't listen, write them a letter—DON'T WHINE!

Besides skiing, Sarah likes to collect "things with cats on them" and American Girl dolls. She and her brother, Jeff, 13, live in Aloha, Oregon. Jeff has mental retardation and epilepsy.✵

✵ *Find out what epilepsy is on page 109!*

Helen Rittelmeyer, 10

I guess I'm glad to have a sister with special needs. It has opened my eyes to a world of people I never would have known about. But, not having special needs myself, it adds stress to what would otherwise be a normal sibling relationship—which is rough just by itself.

Sometimes I wish I had special needs. I think that a lot when Martha gets ooohed and aahed over and nobody even thinks about me. My parents give Martha all the attention and give her all the toys she wants when I barely get anything. Personally, I don't see anything particularly interesting about being mentally retarded. And my parents think that just because Martha has special needs, she can't ever learn that hitting and fussing like an elephant is wrong.

But I have gotten lots of opportunities from Martha. Without her, I never would have started Kids Together, which is a non-profit organization. Kids Together has an annual bazaar to raise money for a handicapped-accessible park in Cary, North Carolina. Many good things have happened because of Martha, so I guess it evens up with the bad things.

Another thing is that it really makes me mad when kids slap their chest with their hands and go, "I'm a retard!" One day that happened in the lunchroom in

2nd grade. And let me tell you, it is *very* loud in the lunchroom. Yet I could still hear a kid saying, "Hey look, I'm a retard!" It made me so mad! But with my anger is also pity that those people will never know what neat people retarded people can be.

Helen, who lives in Cary, North Carolina, likes playing her guitar, reading, and solving logic puzzles. Her sister, Martha, is 7 and has severe mental retardation and seizures. ✺

✺ *Seizures, page 112.*

Chelsea Brown, 11

When my brother, Justin, was born no one was sure what he had, but now doctors think he has Mohr syndrome.✸ Mohr syndrome is very rare. Only an estimated 200 kids in the world have it. Doctors are not sure how long Justin will live. At times I get very scared that he might not live very long.

I try to spend as much time with him as possible, but it is often hard because he is so loud! If you are embarrassed about having a brother or sister with special needs, don't be! I think you should be proud.

At school there was a song going around about children with special needs. The song had a rather harsh word in it! A teacher heard the song and said not to sing it because there are really people with special needs. There is a girl in my grade who respects my feelings. She's one of my best friends. She doesn't use the harsh word because she thinks my brother is really neat, and when she grows up she wants to teach deaf kids.

My other advice for younger brothers or sisters is that if you ever have someone come over, first make sure they understand about your brother or sister and treat your brother or sister completely normal. Also, find out what you should do in case of an emergency.

✸ *Mohr syndrome is described on page 110.*

43

I think my brother really understands my family—
and we understand him. We "talk" even though the
noises Justin makes sound like squeals. I think his
noises really do mean something. My brother does not
go to school with me or my other brother, but he used
to come to school to help the kids in my class understand that he is normal too!

Chelsea's interests include horseback riding, friends,
and sports. Her brother, Justin, is 14. The Browns live
in Holland, Michigan.

Matt Sochia, 11

When I found out that Amy has Down syndrome★ I didn't really care because I was young and I didn't even know her. But now I'm gentle with her because she acts fragile and cries a lot and I don't like getting headaches! I'm really glad Amy's a little different from everyone else. We do lots of things together. I have more fun with her than with most of my friends! Amy cannot go to my school because there is no therapy where I go to school.

★ *Down syndrome, see page 108.*

My parents ask me not to treat her like a baby all of the time. My advice for younger kids is to treat your brothers or sisters correctly and nicely and also patiently. Amy is a little different from everyone else because she talks a little different and a few other things, but other than that, she's perfect.

45

Matt lives in Carthage, New York and enjoys collecting cards and playing sports. To read what his sister Stephanie wrote, turn to page 17.

Stephanie Hodge, 11

I have two siblings who have special needs. My sister Emily, who is 13, has mental retardation. My brother Patrick, who is 10, has Tourette syndrome.✹

✹ What's Tourette syndrome? Find out on page 112.

Here are some of the "good parts" about having siblings with special needs: they make me laugh and I can boss them around! My sister looks up to me and feels my opinions are important.

Here are the "not-so-good parts" of having siblings with special needs: they mess up my room and embarrass me in public places and when I am with my friends. My brother has Tourette syndrome and says bad words that he can't control. Sometimes I feel it's unfair because there are times I wish I could say what he says! My sister gets angry and she hits my friends at lunch when we are at school.

On weekends I get to go to grandma's house. This makes me feel special and gives me a break away from my sister and brother. One year we all went to Hershey park. I had lots of fun riding the roller coaster with my brother, but my sister cried. Next time she'll stay with Mom.

47

When we were younger my mom told me that Emily had a handicap. I wasn't sure what that meant. As we got older Emily still acted like a little kid and I didn't understand. Then mom took me to the library and got me a book about a girl who had a brother who was mentally retarded. When I read the book I knew exactly why my sister was like she was. The book explained everything I needed to know.

My brother has Tourette syndrome and mom took him to the doctors and came home and explained to me that he couldn't stop the weird noises that he makes. I understood more about it when she showed me a videotape about it. In our neighborhood I have friends who are siblings of special needs kids.

Stephanie lives in Carthage, New York, and likes art, reading, and swimming.

Alisha Axman, 11

I have a brother who is six years old and his name is Jared. He has Angelman syndrome.✸

My life has changed in many different ways. I can't have friends over all the time, especially when my brother is sick. I have to help a lot to take care of my brother. Because of my brother, we can't always do things as a family.

The way I learned about Angelman syndrome was from my mom. After doing a lot of research, she sat down and explained what Angelman syndrome is about and what we should expect.

This year, Jared is in kindergarten. He really likes school! He does pretty good, but needs lots of help because he can't talk. We don't know if Jared will ever talk, but we are all learning sign language, which is really fun.

However, it's not always fun having a special needs brother. He embarrasses me in public sometimes when he screams real loud. When he gets sick, I have to be real quiet.

I feel like it is easier being an older sister to a special needs brother, because I understand more about what is going on. If I were younger than him, I wouldn't understand everything that had to do with him.

✸ Learn more about Angelman syndrome by turning to page 106!

I think parents should make sure they spend time and do fun things with the brothers and sisters, and let them know that they are just as special as the special needs siblings. In fact, everyone should treat every kid as if they were very special, whether they have special needs or not.

I love my brother very much and I would not trade him for anyone else!

50

Alisha likes to draw and play basketball. She and Jared, 6, live in Lawrence, Kansas.

Crystal Marie Kirstein, 11

I would just like to say that my Mom and little sister are both disabled and, yes, it is hard but I love them both.

My mom has a visual impairment and epilepsy, which causes her to have seizures. My sister, Melissa, has Down syndrome, also known as Trisomy 21. ✦ Sometimes Melissa is very hard to live with but I wouldn't trade her in for a normal sister any day! She was given to my family for a reason. I don't know the reason, but that's fine.

I feel that people with disabilities are treated OK, although I have seen some treated HORRIBLY!! Just because you have a disability doesn't mean you are bad or anything. One day, the three of us were walking and some high schoolers started teasing my mom and sister. My mom and my sister ignored them, but I didn't! It really bothered me. Most of my friends understand about my mom and my sister. They just leave them alone.

✦ Epilepsy, see page 109; Down syndrome, see page 108.

51

Crystal's interests include her friends, reading, and dancing. She and Melissa, 9, live in Vancouver, Washington.

Lauren Siber, 11

My brother Jason has Down syndrome.✵ This means he does stuff slower and learns slower. He can speak, but not that well. If you have a sibling with Down syndrome you should put in extra time to help him.

Jason gets along with everybody. In most ways, he is not any different than anyone else. Jason is extremely fun to play with. A lot of people think he's bad. I don't. I'm not just saying that because he's my brother. I am saying that because I can judge him. I judge him by how he plays with his friends.

Jason's Down syndrome does not affect me. To me it doesn't matter that he has Down syndrome. I love my brother for who he is and would love him even if he did not have Down syndrome.

Lauren and her brother Jason, 7, live in Manalapan, New Jersey. Lauren likes to play soccer.

✵ *Down syndrome, see page 108.*

Justin Mann, 12

Hi everyone! My name is Justin. I'm 12 years old and in 7th grade. I live at home in New Jersey with my mom and my dad. My sister, Jennifer, is 10 years old. She has hydrocephalus✶ (too much fluid in her brain) and lots of learning problems.

Jennifer also used to have a lot of problems with her behavior. She was always trying to hurt herself and no one could figure out why. Because of this, Jen needed special treatment. She needed someone working with her all of the time to keep her from hurting herself. It was impossible for Jen to live at home. My mom and dad and I could never work with her all the time. I wouldn't get my homework done, my dad wouldn't be able to go to work, and my mom would never have time to shop, make dinner, clean, or drive me to basketball and soccer practice.

Jennifer used to live at a place that was five hours away. It was a good school, but when I was 5 it was upsetting when my mom left to visit Jen. After a while, I learned to handle it okay. It's just the way things are in my house.

Now Jennifer lives in place called Bancroft—a really great school near where we live. She has learned so much in a short time! Her behavior prob-

✶ Hydrocephalus, see page 110.

53

lems are under control and now she can feed herself!
Also, she has learned to walk with a walker—something the doctors said was impossible when she was
born. She still can't talk, but she has learned hand
signs to let you know what she wants.

Because Bancroft is so close we see her two or
three times a week and sometimes we go to the park
or the mall. Sometimes people stare at her. When I
was younger, someone stared at her in a restaurant. I
was sad because that guy thought she
was different from other people.
Now I've learned that
everybody's differ-
ent and it's
okay. So it
doesn't
bother me
when
people
stare. Jen
didn't
cause her
problems and

she can't stop it. I didn't cause it and no one else did either. It's just something that happened. So differences are okay.

I love Jen, but I don't really miss her when she's at school. I guess that's because I'm used to the way things are and I'm busy with school and with my friends. I worry about her though, when she is hurt, has surgery, or has to be in the hospital. If Jen was at home, I would have to help my mom more and I wouldn't have as much spare time. But if she was at home, I suppose I'd be used to that too!

As you can see things are different in my family. Things are the way they are because they have to be. We're still a family and we love each other very much!

55

Justin lives in Marlboro, New Jersey, and enjoys sports, computers, and music.

Jaci Raia, 12

The good part of having a brother with special needs is that no matter what you do to them, they'll always love you. My brother, Brian, is sometimes very caring and other times quite ignorant. Sometimes on rainy days, we play something like office, and we have a blast! And he is very considerate and helpful. He may get a glass if you need one, and remind you to close the cabinet door so you don't bang your head. Brian is always willing to play with me.

Some of the bad parts about having Brian as a sibling are that he hogs the TV, he makes fun of me, and he is just plain ANNOYING! He always teases me and when someone visits, he sticks to me like he's my shadow. And he does some disgusting things that make me sick.

Since I have Brian as a brother, my life is a little different. People want to make it up to Brian because he doesn't have things that normal kids have, like regular speech. So, once in a while, my parents buy him things he wants that aren't too expensive. Once we were in the mall and he saw a little toy train he wanted. My mom bought it for him. Usually when she buys him something, she buys me a little something to try not to make me feel bad. So I asked her if I could get something and she said, "No, I don't have any money left." She had spent it all on Brian! I got really mad then. I wanted to take Brian's new toy and break it, but I didn't because I knew I would get into trouble.

Some changes I'd like my parents to make for me are to STOP comparing me to him. My parents keep going on endlessly about how he can't do certain things, he can't talk right, and on and on and on. Another thing is to stop spending so much time with Brian. I feel ignored a lot. And I want my parents to stop pitying Brian! If he does something bad, he gets yelled at. Then if he starts to cry, my parents rush to him and say, "Aw, what's the matter, Brian?" But if I get yelled at and start to cry, they don't even care. They just say, "Stop it, Jaci. There's no reason you should be acting like a 2 year old." It's always the little things that get me mad.

✸ *Fragile X syndrome is defined on page 109!*

58

Jaci, 12, likes to read and draw. Her brother Brian, 11, has fragile X syndrome.✸ *They live in Edison, New Jersey.*

Michelle Newman, 12

Ever since I was two, I have been living with someone who is different than most people. My sister, Stacy, was born with Trisomy 9 Mosaic.✵ She had to stay in the hospital a little longer than most babies.

✵ *What's Trisomy 9 Mosaic? Find out on page 113!*

After ten long years, I am used to my sister. Some people might think that I probably would like to get rid of her, although I don't know what I would do without her. Even if I had the chance to make her normal I would not change anything. I love her just the way she is.

There are many things that she likes. Her favorite things are: her dad's old T-shirts, balls, swings, and slides. Her favorite people are me and her dad. If my dad or I walk by and we don't take her with us she will start crying! She also likes to pull people's hair and untie their shoelaces. She doesn't like many things other kids like. She doesn't like going to the mall or watching TV. She doesn't stay still for very long and likes to go outside and play with her dog.

It can be hard to live with Stacy. Like when she wakes me up real early or keeps dumping things on the floor. Also, there are things I can't do with her. I can't go to the movies with her or go to places where you sit the whole time.

But there are some good things about Stacy, like her stroller/ wheelchair and being able to use handicapped parking! There are other things that are nice, too. Just looking at her after she eats always makes me laugh. She makes a huge mess! And she always makes me happy. I make her laugh just by doing a somersault or making a silly face.

There isn't much more that I can tell you except that I love her and I love living with someone different.

Michelle lives in Van Nuys, California, and likes to ride her bike and swim. Her sister, Stacy, is 10.

Joe Hockaday, 12

Having a brother with special needs makes my life different from others because he likes to follow me everywhere—even to the bathroom sometimes!

He gets mad at the smallest things. Sometimes he hits himself in the head and that scares me. Sometimes he hits me for no reason.

Sometimes he can be in a bad mood, but we have fun too. We like to laugh and talk and play like other brothers. My friends are really nice to him.

My advice is to respect your sib and treat him like everybody else. Try to understand his needs.

My best time with my brother is when we go to the desert and ride our dirt bike. He doesn't ride by himself so sometimes he rides with me and that makes him happy and me too.

61

Joe lives in Whittier, California, and likes building models and riding his dirt bike. His brother, Bobby, 10, has mild mental retardation.

Allison Hansen, 12

Hi! My name is Allison Hansen. My older brother had a heart transplant in 1994. When I was told he needed a transplant, I didn't know what to feel. I had mixed emotions. My brother was in the hospital for 53 days. I almost never saw my parents except for in the morning, and sometimes at night before I went to bed. This year, my brother and I go to the same school. I don't think my life is any different from other kids my age, because I'm not the one who had the heart transplant. But some kids tease me about my brother. I also don't like it when they always ask "how is your brother?" and never ask about how I am.

One good thing about having a brother with special needs is that I get to learn about the body and the hospital. I also get included in some of the parties my brother goes to, and I get to celebrate that my brother is alive. The bad thing is all the attention he gets. Sometimes I feel left out. People think of me as "Jacob's Sister," and sometimes I don't feel like I get enough attention from my family.

I am 18 months younger than my brother. I think that if he was younger than me, I would understand everything better. I feel like my brother really grew more mature after his transplant, and I know he went through a lot. I've been to a Sibshop✸ before and it really made me feel SPECIAL.

I think brothers and sisters need to be noticed more. We are special too. My advice to others like me is that you always need to remember that your parents love you, no matter how left out you feel. Your special needs sibling needs the special attention at that time. If you need to spend more time with your parents, tell them. I strongly encourage you to attend a Sibshop because they really make you feel important. Also, don't be angry at your brother or sister just because they need extra attention. Be happy that they are still living.

✸ Sibshop, see page 112.

Allison likes to act, sing, and collect key chains. Her brother, Jacob, is 14. The Hansens live in Everett, Washington.

Diana Lowe, 13

Sometimes, there are not-very-good things about having a sibling with special needs. I have a sister with Down syndrome✱ named Katie. She is a really good sister but sometimes I wish she didn't have special needs. One time last week my friend and I were going to go to the movies. Well, my mom asked me if Katie could come with me and my friend. I said "no" because would you want your sister hanging around you if you were going out with your friend? So my mom started to cry and thought that I was so selfish. Then my dad started to yell at me saying I was "so selfish" and that "your mother works so hard to get Katie included and her own sister won't take her to the movies." I was so mad! I tried to explain to them that the only reason I said "no" was because I wanted to be with my friends—not because I was embarrassed to be seen with her! So I ended up taking her with me. But I learned to tell my mom *why* I don't want Katie hanging around all the time. So now we have a better understanding about what we both feel.

✱ Down syndrome, see page 108.

65

Diana likes to hang out with her friends in Warwick, Rhode Island. Her sister, Katie, is 15.

Jeanne Marie Pinto, 13

A person's life can be very different when they live with someone with special needs. I am one of them. My older brother, Carl, who is currently twenty-four years old, is developmentally disabled. He was born that way. He also has mental retardation. The definition of mental retardation is a limitation of intelligence due to the lack of normal mental development rather than to a mental disease or deterioration. There are many people who are developmentally disabled that can carry on a normal everyday life. My brother is not one of them. Even though Carl may look normal, he cannot read or write, he is sometimes very hard to understand, and he speaks in sentence and word fragments. Carl functions like a 4-year-old and will always remain that way.

Having an older brother with special needs makes you creative but it can also be hard to deal with. For instance, if my family and I wanted to go out to eat or to a store we could not go without bringing my brother along—something that you would not want to do! If he saw a clock you would practically have to drag him out of the store since he loves clocks. On the other hand, he can do some pretty interesting things like being able to tell time—even though he cannot read.

I remember one time when I was younger that I invited a friend over. It was one of the times that my brother did not have to go to school for some reason. Carl would always like to bother any girl who would come over to our house. Anyway, my mother promised me she would keep him out of the basement that day so we could have some peace and quiet. At one point she must have turned her back because Carl came downstairs. My friend was not used to his behavior and got scared. She then went back home. I was not very happy.

Ever since that happened I have given a brief talk to my classmates almost every year about my brother and what he is like. Because of this, they understand how I feel. They are also aware of him, so that event would hopefully not be recreated. Doing this also makes me feel better.

My classmates have not really been a problem. Actually, when I was in the fourth grade someone asked me if they could meet him. I had to say no because, knowing my brother, he would disturb the whole school with his constant chatter. He was at his own school at that time.

About a year ago we watched a video on disabilities at school. Many of the kids who laughed knew my

brother personally. This really annoyed me! Also, when
I got an award from WORC (Working Organization for
Retarded Children and Adults) for doing volunteer
work, some of my classmates made it sound like it was
a disease that I had helped out.

My brother has made me upset at times—such as
when my friend had to leave, or when he hit or kicked
me. But there have been many times I have been proud
to have him as a brother. At his graduation when he
was 21, he got an award for being the "most inquisi-
tive." (He asks the same questions over and over
again!) When he participated in Special Olympics, he
would win either first, second, or third place almost
every year. He plays basketball very well.

My brother can also drive you crazy. He enjoys
listening to cassette tapes. When he finds one section
that he likes he will play it over and over again for many
days. One day we gave him a new Sesame Street tape.
That night when my father came home from work, my
mother, my other older brother Chris, and I greeted him
at the door singing "The Lady-bug Picnic." We had
listened to that song many, many times!

About three years ago, Carl moved to a place called
a group home. A group home is one type of place where

adults with disabilities live. My brother was on a waiting list since he was about 10 and it was not until he was 21 that he moved. He moved to WORC's Geraldo Rivera residence. His residence was the first group home established in New York State. My brother Chris says that living in a group home is better than living in a college dorm. People at Carl's house are always either going to the movies, going bowling, going to the disco, etc. He could never have done this if he was still at home. They are always kept busy. Carl's residence consists of 8 people—6 boys and 2 girls—who are a lot like him. With so many new friends and activities, he's frequently not there. Living in a group home has made us happier and he enjoys it. (He proudly calls it "Carl's home.") It has worked out for the best.

Carl has had his good times and his bad times in my memories but no matter what, there will always be a place for him in my heart.

Jeanne lives in Hollis Hills, New York, and enjoys reading, crafts, and music.

Justin Boraas, 13

My name is Justin. My little brother, Mike, has Pervasive Developmental Disorder.★

When he was little, I was the only one who knew what he was saying or what he meant. When he was 3, I helped him learn his abc's and to say words the correct way. When he was 5 he got his first bike, but it came without training wheels. He tried to ride it but he fell off, so I sat on the bike with him and steered and balanced it. At 6, he was having to help a lot more around the house than he wanted. I helped him through that too.

When Mike was four he was scared about monsters and the boogeyman. And when he was 7, he came home pale-white, scared to death of dying. Every day he would come up to me and say, "Justin, am I going to die?" And every day I would say the same thing: "Only if God wants you to." It took two

71

★ *Pervasive Developmental Disorder is described on page 111!*

months for Mike to get over death. I had him talk to Sunday school teachers, ministers—the whole works.

When he got over with that, for some reason he got to think he could do whatever he wanted. If he didn't get his way, he would just throw a fit!

Now he's 9 years old. So far so good. He is totally against smoking or other drugs. That's good, because I smoked for a while and hated it very much.

Mike has a lot of hopes for his future. He has 6 good friends—me, Nick (our older brother), Mom, Dad, the neighbor Erick, and last but not least God. Mike used to have seven friends but one died of cancer. Mike is still getting over it with my help.

Thank you for letting me get this off my chest. I hope people can read this to help them understand siblings.

Justin lives in Benson, Minnesota, and likes wood working and riding his bike. His brother, Mike, is 9.

Derek Urban, 13

My brother, Todd, is 17. When I was 3 my parents explained that he has autism and this was why he couldn't speak and act like other kids. The nice part about having a brother with special needs is that he is happy to go anywhere and do just about anything with me. But sometimes he does bad things like flipping over furniture and writing on the wall. A couple years ago he flipped over our TV unit—with a TV set, CD player, amplifier, and VCR! Then he went through another phase where he was hitting people.

✺ *Autism, see page 106.*

I think my brother will come live with me when my parents can't take care of him. He is older than me, but because he has autism, I think we spend more time together than we would if he didn't have autism. In school some of the mean kids call him a retarded freak but most feel sympathetic. I think that everybody should treat him like a normal person. Even though he has autism I still love him a lot.

73

Derek, who lives in Munhall, Pennsylvania, enjoys building models and robots. To see what his brother Brandon wrote, turn to page 15.

Anne Meade, 14

Hello, my name is Anne Meade and I have a twelve-year-old brother named Michael. He has cerebral palsy.✳ Some people may think having a brother with a disability is fun but it's not all fun and games! Oh, sure, it's great when I can yell at him and he can't yell back or when my family waits in line at a historical place and we get to go to the front of the line to use the elevator.

✳ *Cerebral palsy, see page 107.*

But there are some bad things, too. Like when he can't tell me what's wrong, or when people stare at him, or when he doesn't understand when we want him to do something.

75

Life is sometimes frustrating for the whole family. Sometimes I wonder what my brother is thinking. When he yells, is it a cry of pain or anger or maybe even joy? I get jealous sometimes—I think everybody with a disabled sibling does. So much money is spent on his equipment, but when I want something, I have to use my own baby-sitting money. I understand why he can't buy his own things but it still makes me mad.

I lead a pretty regular life. All my friends love my brother. If I was friends with somebody who didn't like him, I don't know if I would be friends with them anymore. When I baby-sit my brother, sure I may have to change a diaper or two but it's really easy.

Usually, innocent little me, I take over the TV but when his crying becomes intolerable, I usually change the channel.

To end this, I just want to tell all people, young and old, to please resist the urge to stare at people who have disabilities. I do sometimes but after a while, I regret it. And don't take pity on my family! We are normal! Just because my brother has cerebral palsy doesn't mean we are aliens or anything! We have feelings, a brain, and a heart just like every other person in this world. So does my brother!

Anne lives in Sanford, Maine, where she likes to ride horses and hang out with her friends.

Katie Suwala, 14

My name is Katie Suwala and I am 14 years old. My brother, Jason, who is 18, was born with a chromosomal abnormality which left him blind, deaf, short, and mentally retarded. Jason almost died a few times because he became dehydrated. Even though I was only four years old, I was really scared and worried.

Jason is totally dependent on someone to take care of all his needs. Someone has to watch him all the time so he doesn't get hurt when he is on the floor or in his walker. He has some cool equipment such as a swing in his room, a mobile stander, and a scooter so he can move around the floor and bang up the walls!

It's fun to listen to the different sounds Jason makes—he learns new sounds every day. Jason is also learning to sit longer and to roll on the floor more. It's good to have Jason around, because in a lot of ways, it is like having a little baby brother to take care of.

Even our dog, Penny, loves Jason. When Jason's on the potty or on the floor, Penny lays right beside him. Sometimes Jason will pet her.

I like to visit Jason's school because they treat my brother like he's a part of the family. It doesn't even seem like a school because he has so much fun and they keep him busy.

I also like it when Jason comes to my basketball games. When I get frustrated during the game, all I do is look over at his happy face and I feel better.

When I was in fourth grade, we had to write about our best friend. I wrote about Jason and what a great brother he is. I called us twins, because we are the only ones in the family with brown hair, and our teeth are crooked in the same way. My essay took third place! In sixth grade, we had to write about three wishes and one of mine was that Jason was a normal boy. I took third place once again.

I have a best friend and she always asks how Jason is doing. When she comes to our house, she pays attention to him and talks to him like he's no different than anyone else. I also have a friend who has an older sister with special needs and she doesn't treat her sister very well. I feel bad because her sister is very nice and likes to hug people. Still another friend has a newborn baby sister who has special needs. She treats her sister the way I treat my brother.

Having a brother like Jason makes me realize that I am lucky to have such a nice brother. It also makes me appreciate that I don't have all his problems.

78

Katie, who lives in Ford City, Pennsylvania, enjoys volleyball, basketball, and softball. To see what her sister, Lizzie, wrote, turn to page 23.

Severn Kraut, 14

I think my life is different than other kids because we can't do stuff as a family like going on trips or to fairs or fancy restaurants. A good thing about having a sib with special needs is that your brother or sister won't yell at you or mistreat you. And, you can always wrestle them—that's the really good part!!

I have one more comment: When we go places people stare at us; sometimes we feel like telling them to go to the "HOT" place below us. My big hope is when I'm all grown up people will treat the people with disabilities just like they treat other "normal" people.

Severn lives in Camas, Washington, and likes basketball, art, and music. His brother, Lewis, is 11 and has autism. ✹

✹ *Autism, see page 106.*

79

Amy Pogue, 14

Sometimes I get annoyed with people because they don't know what it's like having a sister like Jeannie. Sometimes I help my Mom by watching Jeannie when we're at the grocery store. Occasionally Jeannie throws a temper tantrum, she'll lie on the floor, and usually take a shoe off and throw it. When she does this I get really nasty looks from people, as if I was beating up my innocent little sibling.

Don't get me wrong, she can be real sweet, too. Sometimes I'll read her a book and she'll be real nice and peaceful. Other times she'll pinch and be a brat. One time I was watching Jeannie and she started yelling "hit again, hit again," and I hadn't even touched her! So sometimes I end up with a bum rap.

I try to help my parents. I know that I'll grow up and go away but they will still have to take care of Jeannie. I'll watch her or play with her so they can do something else. She likes to play in our treehouse. We also play on the computer or look at pictures because she loves pictures.

It can be stressful sharing a room. She can't go to sleep until late sometimes, which keeps me up. I have to get up at 6:20; she gets up at 7:20.

I'm also Jeannie's "translator." She talks in short sentences or phrases and sometimes people can't

81

understand, even my parents! Sometimes they say, "Amy, do you know what she's saying?" Jeannie and I have a special bond. I can usually understand her just as well as my Mom and Dad, and sometimes better.

I grew up with Jeannie being like she is and, because I don't have any other brothers or sisters, I'm used to her. My friends wonder how I can keep sane. After almost nine years of living with her (she's nine and I'm fourteen) you get accustomed to living with a person like that.

My life is different from other kids around me. I don't get to have people come over that often because Jeannie is kind of a hassle and I don't live near many kids my age. Sometimes when friends come over they think she's strange—it all depends on her mood. I wouldn't want her to go to my school. She likes where she goes to school. Besides, if she went to my school she wouldn't get the special attention she needs to learn.

All in all, I wouldn't change things. I just hope that she does the best she can.

Amy lives in New Winsdor, New York, and likes to paint. Her sister has mental retardation.

Joshua Kaplan, 16

My name is Josh Kaplan. My brother, Zachary, is 6 years old, and has an "autonomic nervous system disorder."* Since I'm 16, there's a 10-year gap between me and my brother. It's amazing to me how one day I'm swimming in the pool with Zach and the next day I get a call saying that Zach was rushed to the emergency room. It occurs to me that I can't comprehend how Zach feels being rushed to the hospital in an ambulance. I know a lot of people, but my little brother shows more courage than anyone I know. He takes all his dramatic experiences in stride.

The reason I'm writing now is that Zach was rushed to the hospital this morning. As I sit here in this empty house, all I can think about is how Zach's doing right now. Sitting alone at night in an empty house must be like sitting in an uncomfortable hospital bed. I try my best to imagine what he must be feeling. The truth is, I can't possibly imagine what it's like for him.

My mom is the director of a preschool that Zachary attends. She also works part-time with teens in a rehabilitation center. Personally, I feel Zach is incredibly lucky to have her as a mother and friend. So am I! Having vast experience with children, my mom takes everything that happens to Zach in a calm and col-

✿ *Autonomic nervous system disorder, see page 107.*

83

lected manner. I want everyone reading this to realize that without my mother, our family would be in pieces. She doesn't know how valuable she is to me, and the rest of my family.

As you've noticed in this paper, I refer to Zachary as my brother. On paper, Zach is actually my half-brother. My mom and dad divorced when I was young, and my mom remarried one of the greatest men I know. Stephen is my step-father, but to me, he's nothing short of a real father. Stephen and my mother, Stephanie, had Zachary on September 9, 1990. My reason for bringing up this topic is I love Zach no matter what the legal term is. To me, he's my REAL BROTHER! Zachary and I have a sister named Arielle. Arielle is 7 years old, and she's the middle child. Although I pick on her a lot, deep down I love her because she's my sister. It's just as tough for Arielle as it is for me, if not tougher. We both have to deal with having a sibling who has special needs.

I have a few words for all the brothers and sisters who have siblings with special needs. First of all, remember to tell your brother or sister with special needs how much you care. So I say, let them know. Second, your parents love all of you equally, so don't question their love for you. Third, sometimes it will feel like you're not getting any attention. Believe me, your parents don't mean to neglect you. I'm speaking from experience. They always make it up to you. Finally, stay strong and hang in there. I'll end with my parents' two greatest quotes: One, "don't fret the small stuff," and, two, "it's all small stuff!"

Joshua lives in Scottsdale, Arizona. His interests include snowboarding and golf. To read what his sister, Arielle, wrote, turn to page 8.

Megan Patterson, 17

I was so excited when my mom was pregnant. I had it all planned out. The baby would be a girl, and I could dress her up, have tea parties with her, and fix her hair. She would be my baby.

Well, the months passed and my mom had the baby. She called me to tell me that my little sister was, in fact, my little brother. To say the least, this did not thrill me! I remember dropping the phone and running into my grandparents' room. Later that night, my dad came home and told us about Andy. I started not to mind the boy part so much—I figured I could just dress him up like a girl.

On the following day, my grandparent's house was very quiet and everyone was upset. Dad came home and told me that Mommy and Andy would not be home for a while. When I asked why, he just said that Andy was a little sick. He made me promise that I would not worry. He said that mom, the doctors, and he would take good care of Andy.

I finally saw Andy when he was well enough for visitors. I thought he was the largest, ugliest thing alive! You see, he was in a room with the premature babies and had a rash from the tape he had on his face and arms. Having Down syndrome✦ and a heart condition, Andy was a sick little baby.

✦ *Down syndrome, see page 108.*

87

After Andy was born, my life and my outlook changed forever. I was no longer the baby of the family, so my older brother and sister threw me a party welcoming me into the "big brothers and big sisters club." Andy was in the hospital a lot with pneumonia and his heart. Because of this, I spent a lot of time at my Grammie's house. This was a lot of fun, but I missed my mom.

I became a more accepting person after the birth of Andy. It used to bother me when people would stare at him, and sometimes it still does. I became more accustomed to seeing people with disabilities and not staring like I did before. Today, I see Andy as a totally typical kid, not as a kid who needs a lot of help, or even as a kid with Down syndrome.

Because of Andy, I have learned how to cope with things in my life. When my Grammie died, we were all upset, although Andy did not exactly understand death. At the funeral home, Andy stood just outside the room where Grammie was, surrounded by many of her proper friends. And then he said something which cannot be repeated and made everyone laugh. Grammie would have liked that.

My friend, John, died the summer before my junior year. Andy helped me through that too when he said, "Don't cry Meg, you'll make John sad. He doesn't want to see you cry."

Every day Andy teaches me to never give up. He knows he is different, but he doesn't focus on that. He doesn't give up, and every time I see him having a hard time, I make myself work that much harder. He teaches me to be dedicated to my work and to be proud of all I do, just as he is.

I don't know what I would do without Andy. He changed my life, my family's, and my friends', who treat him like a normal kid. If I had not grown up with him, I would have less understanding, patience, and compassion for people. He shows us that anyone can do anything.

Now I look at Andy at age eleven. He goes to the same school that I went to and has the same teachers I had. I stand back and watch, still learning from him every day.

Megan lives in Mentor, Ohio, and likes children, animals, and spending time with her friends.

89

Kate Turnbull, 18

He walks funny, as walks go, I suppose. He twitches his fingers whenever he stares at that interesting nothingness on the wall, which the rest of us cannot see. He asks God to bless all the good people when he says his prayers at night. He plants his feet on the dance floor and moves his hips back and forth when he dances at the local jazz bar. He can write only his first name. He thinks M&M's and a house cost the same: $100. He has taught me about the human capacity for love, acceptance, and friendship. He has autism✸ and mental retardation. He is my brother, J.T. Turnbull.

✸ *Autism, see page 106.*

I do not remember a moment when my parents set me down and told me about J.T.'s disabilities. I always knew he was different.

I do, however, remember the early disillusioning experiences of prejudice and discrimination when J.T. was laughed at, ridiculed, and shunned because of his differences. Because of this, I have spoken out for my brother and people like him at local, national, and international conferences on the family and disability ever since I was seven years old. I even reported a special education teacher to the principal when I was in sixth grade because I witnessed her abuse a peer with a disability. J.T.'s struggle did not embitter me—on the contrary, it empowered me.

When I was younger, my parents struggled to get J.T. and other people with disabilities included in "regular" classes at the local high school. They were told that they were crazy. I remember how, following high school, they tried to find places for my brother to live and work in the community—something other than group homes and sheltered workshops. "They are not part of the community living and working this way." my parents said. "They are not being treated as full citizens." My parents were laughed at.

Achieving their dreams for J.T. wasn't easy. J.T. had behavior problems, which included anything from choking to hair-pulling to hitting. After being asked to leave a group home, J.T. moved back in with my parents who "hired" a friend for him—J.T.'s first friend at age 21. Through this friend, J.T.'s circle of friends expanded. Today, he lives in his own house with two graduate students and works at the University of Kansas. It is my parents' advocacy and determination I will always remember.

J.T.'s many accomplishments and my parents' struggle have taught me to have great expectations for *myself.* If J.T., with his problems, can face his challenges with courage and a sense of optimism, then so can I. J.T.'s lesson is a universal one: we all have the capacity for human greatness.

J.T. has taught me about love as well. If a person who was homeless or terminally ill approached J.T., my brother would automatically extend his love and friendship. He would neither see nor understand why this person is different from the rest of us. He would probably ask this stranger to come to his house for lunch and include her in his prayers.

Yes, J.T. has below-kindergarten "intelligence level." And, no, he has never read a book on his own nor has he ever signed his last name. But he naturally understands something that the rest of us do not always recognize: Human beings are human beings and, although people may come from different parts of the world, different socioeconomic classes, and different cultures, we will always have humanity in common. J.T. can make anyone smile when he is smiling. That is the simplest, best reminder of his common touch.

J.T. has taught me about struggle, about empowerment, about beating the odds, and about love. These lessons are valuable to me as I grow up in a world where I turn on the news and see peacemakers assassinated and families and communities despairing over the gang violence that has invaded their towns. I get angry.

But then I look at J.T., sitting in his chair with his legs crossed, gazing at the wall, twitching his fingers and giggling to himself every once in a while. The simplicity of his life, his appreciation for the innate humanity within each person, and his pure, unconditional love are lessons to us all.

Whenever he sees me crying, he asks me, "Katie, are you sad? Oh, let me give you a hug. Things will get better soon." Will they, J.T.? OK, I trust you. **93**

A student at the University of Kansas, Kate loves to act and volunteers at a local free meal program. Her brother, J.T. (Jay Turnbull), is 29.

So What's On Your Mind?

I would very much like to know what you thought of *Views from Our Shoes*. What parts did you like—or not like? Did any of the letters make you think of your life, your sibling, or your family? How? How did it feel to read about the experiences of other brothers and sisters? Are there ways we could make this book better? Write to me at the address below and let me know!

After reading *Views from Our Shoes* you may have thought "*I* would have liked to have written something for this book! If only I had known!" Well, here is your chance. If you would like to write about your experiences I would love to read about them. I can't promise that your essay will end up in a book such as *Views from Our Shoes,* but who knows! I will always ask your (and your parents') permission before I use it in print.

(Of course, you can always write an essay and keep it to yourself or share it with your parents. Writing is a *great* way to figure out how you feel about something!)

Here are some questions to think about when you write your essay. Please remember, these questions are just to get you started—you can write about things that *aren't* on this list. Also, it's better to answer one, two, or maybe three questions than try to answer each question. Please try to write or print your essay as clearly as possible on lined paper. I don't want to mis-quote you! (Of course, you—or a parent—can type if that is easier.)

- ❖ How did you learn about your sibling's disability? How was it explained to you?
- ❖ Is your life very different from other kids in your neighborhood who are your age? How?
- ❖ What are the "good parts" of having a sibling who has special needs?
- ❖ What are the "not-so-good parts" of having a sibling who has special needs?
- ❖ What do you think will happen when you and your brother or sister with special needs grow up?
- ❖ Is being a sister of a kid with special needs different from being a brother of a kid with special needs? How?
- ❖ Is being younger than a child with special needs different from being older than a child with special needs? How?
- ❖ Does your sibling with special needs go to your school?
- ❖ If yes, what do you think about your sib going to your school?

- ❖ Are friends and classmates ever a problem? How do kids in your school treat children who have special needs?
- ❖ Have you been to programs or workshops just for brothers and sisters? What did you think of them?
- ❖ What do you think parents should do for brothers and sisters of kids with special needs?
- ❖ What do you think teachers and doctors and other "professionals" should do for brothers and sisters of kids with special needs?
- ❖ What advice would you give to a younger brother or sister?
- ❖ Do you have a story about your brother or sister or your family that you would like to share? This story can be about almost anything. It can be about a good time, a funny thing that happened with your brother or sister, a not-so-happy time—anything!

Please tell me your age, your birthdate, what grade you are in, and any hobbies or interests you might have. Be sure to let me know your sibling's name, and age. If there is a name for your sibling's special need, please tell me that too. Finally, be sure to include your name, address, and phone number.

I look forward to hearing from you! I think brothers and sisters are the greatest!

All the best,

Don Meyer

Sibling Support Project

Children's Hospital and Medical Center

P.O. Box 5371, CL-09

Seattle, WA 98105-0371

Appendix

If you would like to learn more about some of the special needs mentioned in this book, check out the resources listed below.

A Few Words about the World Wide Web

The Web can be a great place to find out all sorts of information. (If you can't get on the Web at home, try your local library.) Web "search engines" will comb the World Wide Web to find information on just about any topic you can think of—skateboards to seizure disorders and everything in between. The following are some of the most popular engines and their addresses.

Yahoo: http://www.yahoo.com
WebCrawler: http://query.webcrawler.com
Alta Vista: http://www.altavista.digital.com
HotBot: http://www.hotbot.com
Excite: http://www.excite.com

To get to the search engine, start your computer, open your web browser and type in the address. Once your search engine is loaded, simply type the topic you would like to learn more about in the "search box," click "search" and, chances are, you will find lots of information!

There are also many Web Pages regarding disabilities and other special needs. We list some below, but one page deserves special mention: The Family Village Web Site (http://www.familyvillage.wisc.edu) has tons of information on disabilities. Check out their "library" and you might just find what you are looking for. (Much of the information listed below was found at the Family Village library.)

And, while we are on the subject of the World Wide Web, be sure to visit the Sibling Support Project's Web Page (http://www.chmc.org/ departmt/sibsupp). Once you are there, you can check out resources for brothers and sisters and subscribe to SibKids and SibNet. Both SibKids and SibNet are email "listservs" that allow subscribers to meet and write to brothers and sisters from all over the world! And they're free!

ORGANIZATIONS SERVING PEOPLE WITH SPECIAL NEEDS

Below are names, addresses, phone numbers and Web addresses for organizations that can provide you with more information about some of the special needs mentioned in this book.

Angelman Syndrome
Angelman Syndrome Foundation (ASF)
P.O. Box 12437
Gainesville, FL 32604
713-354-7192 or 800-If-Angel
Fax: 713-354-1391

Canadian Angelman Syndrome Society (CASS)
Box 37
Priddis, Alberta T0L 1W0, Canada
403-931-2415
Fax: 403-931-2415

The Angelman Syndrome Web Page:
http://people.zeelandnet.nl/fhof/angelman.htm

Attention Deficit Disorders

CHADD (Children and Adults with Attention Deficit Disorder)
499 N.W. 70th Ave., Suite 101
Plantation, FL 33317
305-587-3700 or 800-233-4050
Fax: 305-587-4599
http://www.chadd.org/

Attention Deficit Disorder Association (ADDA)
P.O. Box 972
Mentor, OH 44061
800-487-2282

Autism

Autism Society of America (ASA)
7910 Woodmont Ave., Suite 650
Bethesda, MD 20814-3015
301-657-0881 or 800-328-8476
Fax: 301-657-0869
http://www.autism-society.org/

Autism Research Institute (ARI)
4182 Adams Ave.
San Diego, CA 92116
619-281-7165
Fax: 619-563-6840

Cerebral Palsy

United Cerebral Palsy Associations, Inc.
1660 L St., NW, Suite 700
Washington, DC 20036-5603
800-872-5827
Fax: 202-842-3519
http://www.UCPA.ORG

American Acad. for Cerebral Palsy and Developmental Medicine
6300 North River Rd .
Suite 727
Rosemont, IL 60018-4226
708-698-1635
Fax: 708-823-0536

Down Syndrome

National Down Syndrome Society (NDSS)
666 Broadway
New York, NY 10012-2317
212-460-9330 or 800-221-4602
Fax: 212-979-287
http://www.ndss.org/

National Down Syndrome Congress (NDSC)
1605 Chantilly Dr., Suite 250
Atlanta, GA 30324
404-633-1555 or 800-2322-6372
Fax: 404-633-2817
e-mail: ndsc@charitiesusa.com
http://members.carol.net/~ndsc/

Canadian Down Syndrome Society
811 14th Street, N.W.
Calgary, AB P2N 2A4
403-270-8500
Fax:403-270-8291

Association for Children with Down Syndrome
2616 Martin Ave.
Bellmore, NY 11710
516-221-4700

Fax: 516-221-4311

E-mail: info@acds.com

Epilepsy and Seizure Disorders

Epilepsy Foundation of America (EFA)

4351 Garden City Drive

Landover, MD 20785-2267

301-459-3700 or 800-332-1000

800-332-2070 TTY

Fax: 301-577-4941

http://www.efa.org/

Fragile X Syndrome

FRAXA Research Foundation, Inc.

P. O. Box 935

West Newbury, MA 01985

508-462-1990

e-mail fraxa@seacoast.com

http://www.worx.net/fraxa/

National Fragile X Association

1441 York St., Suite 215

Denver, CO 80206

303-333-6155 or 800-688-8765

Hydrocephalus

Hydrocephalus Association (HA)

870 Market Street, Suite 955

San Francisco, CA 94102

415-776-4713

http://neurosurgery.mgh.harvard.edu/ha/

Mental Retardation
The Arc
500 East Border St.
Arlington, TX 76010
817-261-6003; 817-277-0553 (TTY)
Fax: 817-277-3491
http://TheArc.org/welcome.html

Rett Syndrome
International Rett Syndrome Association
9121 Piscataway Rd., Suite 2B
Clinton, MD 20735
800-818-7388; Fax: 301-856-3336
http://www.paltech.com/irsa/irsa.htm

Tourette Syndrome
Tourette Syndrome Association (TSA)
42-40 Bell Blvd.
Bayside, NY 11361
718-224-299; Fax: 718-279-9596
e-mail: tourette@1x.netcom.com

The Tourette Syndrome Home Page
http://www.umd.umich.edu/~infinit/tourette.html

Other Disorders
National Organization for Rare Disorders
P.O. Box 8923
New Fairfield, CT 06182-8923
203-746-6518
Fax: 203-746-6481
E-mail: orphan@nord-rdb.com
http://www.pcnet.com/~orphan/

INFORMATION FOR SIBLINGS
Sibshops
Sibshops are fun, lively, pedal-to-the-metal events just for brothers and sisters of kids with special needs. At Sibshops, kids play new games, create art, and cook. They also meet other brothers and sisters and talk about the good and not-so-good parts of having a sibling with special needs. To learn more about Sibshops or where to find a Sibshop or other sibling program near where you live, contact:

> Don Meyer
> Sibling Support Project
> Children's Hospital and Medical Center
> P.O. Box 5371, CL-09
> Seattle, WA 98105-0371
> 206-368-4911
> dmeyer@chmc.org

At the web page (http://www.chmc.org/departmt/ sibsupp) you can find a complete state-by-state listing of all known Sibshops and other sibling programs!

The Sibling Information Network Newsletter
The Sibling Information Network Newsletter is published quarterly and includes information for and about siblings of people with disabilities as well as other issues related to families of people with disabilities. To subscribe, contact:

> Sibling Information Network Newsletter
> A. J. Pappanikou Center
> 249 Glenbrook Rd., U-64
> Storrs, CT 06269-2064

Glossary

Attention Deficit Disorder (ADD)—People who have attention deficit disorder have problems with paying attention, being hyperactive, and/or controlling their impulses. While many kids have problems with paying attention, being hyperactive, and controlling their impulses *some* of the time, people with ADD have trouble *most* of the time. If you want to learn more about ADD, turn to page 101.

turn to page 101.

Angelman syndrome is named after Dr. Harry Angelman. People who have Angelman syndrome often have serious learning problems, a stiff jerky gait, sleep problems, seizures, and do not speak. They often have happy personalities. In 1987, it was discovered that about half of the children with Angelman syndrome have a small piece of chromosome 15 missing. To learn more about Angelman syndrome, turn to page 100.

turn to page 100.

Autism is a lifelong developmental disability that prevents a person from correctly understanding what he or she sees, hears, or senses. This makes communicating and learning difficult. People who have autism often have unusual ways of relating to people and objects. Children with autism may like to be alone or seem like they aren't paying attention. It may seem as if they can't see or hear other people. Some people who have autism flick their fingers or rock back and forth or do other things that seem different. There is much to learn about autism! You can start by checking out the resources on page 101.

Autonomic nervous system disorders affect the brain's ability to control the body functions that we usually don't even think about—swallowing, breathing, motility (the movement of food through our digestive systems), and temperature regulation. Some kids with autonomic nervous system disorders wear apnea monitors which sound an alarm if the child stops breathing. Others who have problems swallowing may need to get their food through a gastrostomy tube (also called a G-tube). Doctors surgically place a G-tube through a hole in the child's abdomen and stomach walls.

Cerebral Palsy—sometimes called CP—is the name given to certain disorders that affect movement. Cerebral palsy can occur when the part of the brain that controls movement is damaged before, during, or soon after birth. The brain ("cerebral") damage can result in poor muscle control ("palsy"). Cerebral palsy can affect how

107

a person walks, sits, eats, writes, and talks. No two people are affected by cerebral palsy in the same way. For some people who have it, cerebral palsy is not very noticeable, while others may be very severely affected. To learn more about cerebral palsy, see page 101. To learn more about seizures, see page 103.

Down syndrome, which is named after Dr. J. Langdon Down, is also known as Trisomy 21. To understand Down syndrome, you must know a little about chromosomes. Most of our cells have 46 chromosomes. To study them, scientists divide the 46 chromosomes into 23 pairs. Most people have a pair of "number 1 chromosomes," a pair of "number 2 chromosomes," and so on—all the way to a pair of "number 23 chromosomes." Someone who has Down syndrome or Trisomy 21 has three "number 21 chromosomes," instead of the usual two.

People with Down syndrome often have speech problems, heart defects, and respiratory problems, and are shorter than other people their age. Many have other physical characteristics, such as upwardly slanted eyes and small ears and noses. Compared to other children, children with Down syndrome are usually slower to learn . To learn more about Down syndrome, turn to page 102.

Epilepsy—People who have epilepsy are people who are likely to have seizures. ***Seizures*** happen when brain cells are abnormally active. Usually, brain cells work just fine. But when a person has a seizure, their brain cells send mixed-up messages for a short while—a few seconds to a minute or two. The mixed-up signals stop the other brain cells from working the right way. As a result, their bodies can get mixed-up messages. People who have seizures may move in ways they don't intend. Their arms or legs may shake. They may smell or hear things that are not there. They may just stop and stare for a short while. There is a lot to learn about epilepsy and seizures! To find out how to learn more, see page 103.

109

Fragile X syndrome is a genetic condition that usually causes mental impairments. These impairments can range from learning disabilities to mental retardation. People who have fragile X syndrome can have autistic-like behaviors (see page 101), very flexible joints, long faces, large ears, and flat feet. Usually, fragile X affects boys more than girls.

People who have fragile X syndrome have a break, or weakness, on the long arm of the X chromosome. (X chromosomes and Y chromosomes are called the sex chromosomes. Males have an X and a Y chromosome. Females have two X chromosomes.) Fragile X is thought to be one of the most common known causes of mental retardation. To learn more about fragile X syndrome, see page 103.

Hydrocephalus comes from the Greek words for water (hydro) and head (cephalus). Hydrocephalus occurs when there is too much cerebrospinal fluid (CSF) within the ventricles of the brain. CSF is produced in the ventricles, cushions the brain and spinal cord, and is absorbed into the bloodstream. Hydrocephalus occurs when the body cannot absorb all the CSF that is produced. When the CSF builds up, it causes the ventricles to enlarge and the pressure inside the head to increase. To release the pressure, doctors insert a tiny tube—called a shunt—into the child's head. The shunt drains the extra CSF from the brain to other parts of the body. To learn more about hydrocephalus, turn to page 103.

Mohr syndrome is named after Otto Mohr, a Norwegian geneticist. Scientists are unsure of what causes Mohr syndrome. People who have Mohr syndrome often have hearing loss, mental retardation, and other problems.

A *Pervasive Developmental Disorder* (PDD) is any one of a group of conditions that interfere with social development, communication, and thinking skills. Although some people who have PDD have mental retardation, others have normal IQs. Autism and Asperger syndrome are two well-known types of PDD. Sometimes, when children have some—but not all—of the signs of a disorder such as autism or Asperger syndrome, they are said to have PDD.

Prader-Willi *syndrome* is named after Swiss pediatricians Andrea Prader and Heinrich Willi. Children who have Prader-Willi often are shorter than other children and have learning, behavior, and weight problems. They also have an almost uncontrollable appetite because their hypothalamuses—the part of the brain that controls hunger and feeling full—don't work right.

Rett *Syndrome* is named after Dr. Andreas Rett of Vienna, Austria. Rett syndrome happens only to girls. Doctors still don't know what causes it. Girls who have Rett syndrome have mental retardation, problems walking and communicating, and seizures. Most lose the ability to use their hands purposefully. To learn more about seizures, see page 103. To find out how to learn more about Rett syndrome, see page 104.

Seizures happen when brain cells are abnormally active. Often, people with epilepsy will have seizures. For more information on seizures, see **epilepsy** on page 109.

Sibshops and other sibling programs are great ways to meet other brothers and sisters! See page 105 to learn more about Sibshops and to find a sibling program near where you live.

112

Supported living is for adults with disabilities who can do many things for themselves. They may live in an apartment or a home with one or several roommates. From time to time, a trained helper will help them with things they can't do for themselves, like housecleaning or paying the bills. *Group homes* often have four to ten adults with disabilities who live together. They are supervised by people who stay at the group home and help take care of the people who live there.

Tourette syndrome is named after a French neurologist, George Gilles de la Tourette. People who have Tourette syndrome frequently have urges to make movements and sounds (called tics) which seem to serve no purpose. Although some people can suppress their tics for a short time, people with Tourette syndrome usually can't control their tics. Doctors think Tourette syndrome results from an imbalance of several chemicals (called neurotransmitters) in the brain. To learn more about Tourette syndrome, see page 104.

Trisomy 9 Mosaic is a very rare condition. There are only a few people in the United States who have this condition. Just as people who have Down syndrome (or Trisomy 21) have three number 21 chromosomes, people who have Trisomy 9 have three "number 9 chromosomes." The word "mosaic" in Trisomy 9 Mosaic means that the person has three number 9 chromosomes in just *some* of her cells. People who have Trisomy 9 Mosaic are small, have mental retardation, and do not talk. To learn more about trisomys and chromosomes, see the description of Down syndrome on page 108.

113

Index

Angelman syndrome, 49-50, 100, 106

Attention Deficit Disorder, 19, 101, 106

Autism, 5, 7, 10, 15, 27-28, 37, 73, 79, 90-93, 101, 106-107

Autonomic nervous system disorders, 8, 83-85, 107

Blindness, 23-24, 77.
   See also Visual impairment

Cerebral palsy, 1-2, 11, 13-14, 29-30, 33-34, 75-76, 101, 107

Chronic lung disease, 1-2

Deafness, 21-22, 23-24, 77

Down syndrome, 17, 25-26, 45, 52, 65, 87-89, 102, 108

Epilepsy, 39, 51, 103, 109.
   See also Seizures

Fragile X syndrome, 57-58, 103, 109

Hydrocephalus, 9, 53-55, 103, 110

Mental retardation, 23-24, 35-36, 39, 41-42, 47-48, 61, 67-70, 77, 81-82, 90-93, 104

Mohr syndrome, 43-44, 110

Pervasive developmental disorder, 71-72, 111. *See also* Autism

Physical disabilities, 21-22

Prader-Willi syndrome, 31-32

Rett syndrome, 3-4, 104, 111-112

Seizures, 1-2, 41-42, 112.
   See also Epilepsy

Sibshops, 25-26, 64, 105, 112

Supported living, 28, 112

Tourette syndrome, 47-48, 104, 112-113

Transplant, 63-64

Trisomy 9 Mosaic, 59-60, 113

Visual impairment, 21-22, 51.
   See also Blindness

About the Illustrator

Cary Pillo has been illustrating for children since 1982. Most of her work concerning children has been in the education, safety, and health related areas. She lives in Seattle, Washington with her husband Jim, nine-year-old son, Seth, and their Fox Terrier, Rocket.